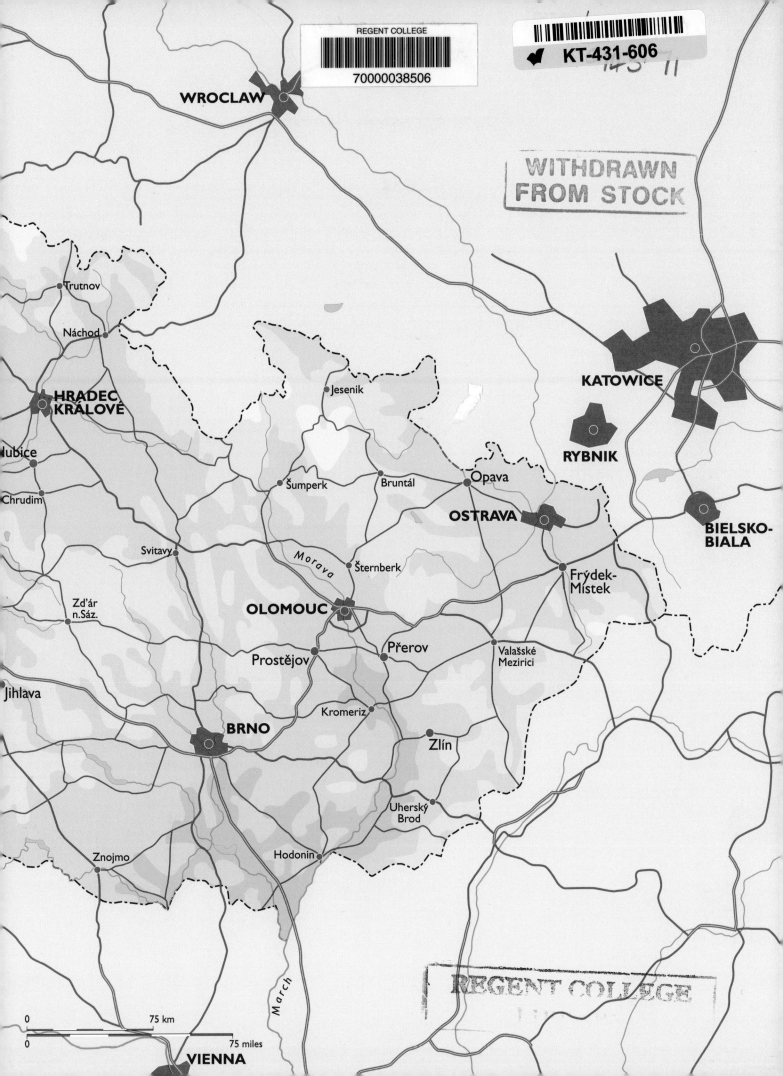

WROCLAW

KATOWICE

RYBNIK

BIELSKO-
BIALA

Trutnov

Náchod

Jesenik

HRADEC
KRÁLOVÉ

ubice

Chrudim

Šumperk

Bruntál

Opava

OSTRAVA

Svitavy

Morava

Šternberk

Frýdek-
Místek

Zd'ár
n.Sáz.

OLOMOUC

Přerov

Valašské
Mezirici

Jihlava

Prostějov

Kromeriz

BRNO

Zlín

Uherský
Brod

Znojmo

Hodonin

March

0

75 km

0

75 miles

VIENNA

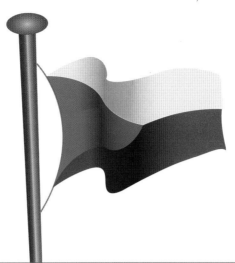

New EU Countries and Citizens

The Czech Republic

Jan Willem Bultje

A Cherrytree Book

This edition published in 2006 by Evans Brothers Limited
2A Portman Mansions
Chiltern Street
London W1U 6NR, UK

Reprinted 2006
Published by arrangement with KIT Publishers, The Netherlands

British Library Cataloguing-in-Publication Data
Bultje, Jan Willem
Czech Republic. - (New EU countries and citizens)
1. Czech Republic - juvenile literature
I. Title
943.7'1
ISBN 1842343254
9781842343258

Text: Jan Willem Bultje
Photographs: Jan Willem Bultje
Translation: Peter Melville
UK editing: Sonya Newland
Design and Layout: Grafisch Ontwerpbureau Agaatsz BNO, Meppel, The Netherlands
Cover: Big Blu Ltd
Cartography: Armand Haye, Amsterdam, The Netherlands
Production: J & P Fast East Productions, Soest, The Netherlands

Picture Credits
All images courtesy of KIT Publishers except:
p. 17(b) © Richard Crawford; Cordaiy Photo Library Ltd./CORBIS;
p. 25 © Liba Taylor/CORBIS; p. 32 © Dave G. Houser/CORBIS

Contents

Introduction

The area that is now the Czech Republic was once divided into two regions – Bohemia and Moravia – and the names of these two parts are still used today. The country has undergone much upheaval throughout its history and it only became an independent state in 1993.

▼ *St Vitus Cathedral is the largest church in Prague.*

The Czech Republic is bordered in the north and west by Germany and in the north-east by Poland. To the south-east lies Slovakia and to the south, Austria. The country is landlocked, and over the years peoples from surrounding European lands have invaded and ruled the area. For many years it was part of the kingdom of Hungary and the powerful Habsburg Empire. For much of the twentieth century the Czech Republic and Slovakia were one country – Czechoslovakia. Because of all this change and the mixture of people who settled in the region, there have been times when the Czech national identity was almost lost. However, the language, culture and traditions of the native peoples were preserved, and experienced a revival in the nineteenth century.

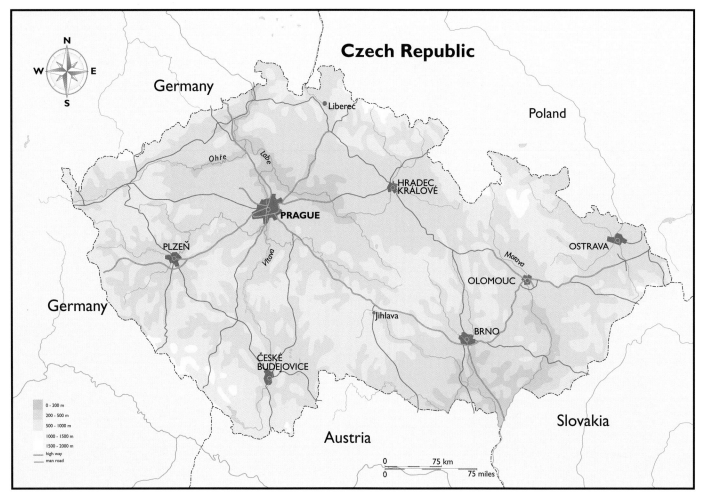

The capital of the Czech Republic is Prague – one of the most beautiful cities in Europe. Every year, thousands of people visit Prague to admire the architecture and enjoy the many sites of this ancient city, which include castles, churches, parks and gardens.

Prague is not the only place to enjoy such sights, though. All across the country, old buildings are carefully preserved or restored, and even in the countryside visitors can experience the wonderful architecture – fairytale castles are scattered all over the country.

The Czech landscape is – like that of many European countries – beautiful and diverse. There are high mountainous regions, perfect for skiing in the winter, and areas of lowland with rivers and lakes. The largest rivers are the Labe and the Vltava, and these have been celebrated in song and story for centuries.

▲ *These wines come from Moravia — the largest wine-producing region in the Czech Republic.*

The Czech Republic became a member of the European Union on 1 May 2004. After centuries of uncertainty, the Czech people hope that this will bring some stability to their country, and allow them to further celebrate their own culture. Belonging to the European Union will help improve foreign policy, economy, and trade and industry in the Czech Republic. The country now enjoys good relations with its neighbouring countries, and also maintains good diplomatic relations with 85 countries worldwide – the majority of which have permanent representatives in Prague. As well as the European Union, the Czech Republic is a member of several other important international organisations, including NATO and the World Trade Organization.

◄ *Ornate gabled houses are a familiar sight in towns and cities all over the Czech Republic. These are in Horovsky-Tyn.*

History

People first settled in the area that is now the Czech Republic in the Stone Age. Celtic tribes lived in the region until around 600 BC. It was the Boii, descendants of the Celts, that gave their name to the part of the country that is now known as Bohemia.

A succession of peoples migrated to this part of Europe after the Celts, including Teutonic tribes and the Romans. The Romans did not settle here for very long, but remains of Roman defence structures can still be seen on the north bank of the River Danube.

In the fifth and sixth centuries AD, Slav peoples moved to this area and drove out the Teutonic tribes. Among these peoples were the Czechs and the Slovenes. The Czech tribes settled in the Vltava river basin and the Slovenian tribes moved a little further to the east.

▼ *Prague is the capital of the Czech Republic. It is situated on the Vltava River.*

◀ *The monastery at Vyšší Brod in the southern Czech Republic.*

Charlemagne

In the seventh century, the Frankish merchant Samo succeeded in uniting the various Slav tribes into one kingdom. A century later, this kingdom fell under the rule of Charlemagne, king of the Franks and Holy Roman Emperor. During Charlemagne's reign, two Greek missionaries – Cyrillus and Methodius – came to this part of Central Europe to teach the people about Christianity. They preached the gospels and many converted to the Greek Orthodox faith. Charlemagne embraced the new religion because it helped to unite different peoples from different tribes and nations.

▼ *Statues of the Greek missionaries Cyrillus and Methodius, who brought Christianity to the region in the late eighth century AD.*

Svatopluk

In the ninth century, the area was ruled by Svatopluk. This great king founded a large empire – Greater Moravia – which not only covered the regions of the Czech Republic and Slovakia, but also stretched far into present-day Poland and Hungary. The Great Moravian Empire grew to be an important European power. After Svatopluk's death, in the tenth century, the kingdom was raided by the Magyars (Hungarians) and the empire began to crumble. The Magyars mainly settled in the area that is now Slovakia. Tribal chiefs from Bohemia asked the Franks for help in defending their country from the Magyars. The most important tribe in Bohemia was the Czechs, and they were granted the power to rule over all the other tribes living there. from this time onwards, all the Bohemian tribes became known as Czechs.

After the collapse of the Great Moravian Empire, the Přemyslide dynasty ruled over the Czechs in Bohemia and the neighbouring region Moravia. Over the next three centuries members of the dynasty considerably extended the Czech territories.

▲ *St Vitus Cathedral in Prague – one of the many magnificent buildings that remain from the time of Charles IV.*

▼ *Prague Castle, originally built in the ninth century, was the seat of power of the Czech rulers throughout the Middle Ages. It was expanded during the time of Charles IV.*

Charles IV

In 1310, the kingdom of Luxembourg took over the Přemyslide possessions. One of the kings from this family, Charles IV, was crowned Emperor of Germany. During his rule, Bohemia enjoyed a period of prosperity. In 1348, Charles IV founded the University of Prague, where lectures were given not only in Latin, but also in German and Czech. Prague became an important city and the emperor invited famous Italian architects, sculptors and painters to build palaces, castles and monasteries all over the city. Many of these can still be seen today.

Under Charles IV, Bohemia became the centre of the Roman-German Empire. However, more difficult times were not far off. Charles's son, Wenceslas IV, was greatly loved by the Czech people, but the nobility and the clergy – mostly of German descent – felt that he focused too much attention on Bohemia and deposed him as Holy Roman Emperor in 1400. Although he remained king of Bohemia, much of the good work done by Charles IV began to disappear. The nobles started to exploit the peasants. The Church began to raise the rent of its estates, on which the poor people lived, and the power and wealth of the Church increased.

▲ *This illustration shows John Huss during his trial in 1414.*

John Huss was born around 1370. He studied law at the University of Prague, became a priest and, in 1402, was made Dean of the University. He was annoyed by the attitude of the Roman Catholic Church, which was increasingly occupied with acquiring power and wealth, rather than with the plight of the people. He started arguing with the Catholic rulers, such as the archbishop, the pope and the German emperor. In 1411, he retired to the country to write books, in which he said that he no longer acknowledged the pope's authority. In 1414, he was called to the town of Constance in Germany, to be put on trial for heresy. He was sentenced to death and burned at the stake on 6 June 1415.

John Huss

Around this time one man led a revolt against the Church, which was growing rich and corrupt. John Huss was Dean of the University of Prague and he began to preach in favour of reform in the country. He wanted the priests – who were living lives of luxury – to return to the old ways. This was very popular with the people, and Huss gathered quite a following. King Wenceslas sympathised with John Huss's ideas, but the Church was very powerful. The pope excommunicated Huss and later had him burnt at the stake for being a heretic.

After his death, Huss's followers, the Hussites, revolted against the German overlords. They demanded a society based on community, with no personal possessions. This struggle, known as the Hussite Wars, went on for several years, ending in 1436.

The Habsburgs

In 1526, Ferdinand I became king of Bohemia. He later became Holy Roman Emperor and was the first Habsburg to rule in Czech lands. He joined Bohemia with Moravia to make them a single province. Throughout the reigns of Ferdinand's successors, Maximillian II and Rudolf II, Czech lands flourished. Rudolf moved his court back to Prague and the city became a centre of learning and culture once again.

The Habsburgs were Catholic, but the majority of Czech nobles were Protestant. When Ferdinand II came to the throne in 1617 he tried to drive the nobles from their lands; the following year this started a conflict that became known as the Thirty Years' War.

▼ *The ascension of Emperor Rudolf II to the Czech throne marked the beginning of the country's second golden age. The emperor made Prague his seat of power, and scientists, artists and writers flocked to the city.*

► *This book tells the story of Frederick von der Pfalz – the 'Winter King'.*

The 'Winter King'

In 1619, the Protestant nobles deposed the Catholic king and elected their own king, Frederick von der Pfalz. Frederick was the grandson of the Dutch governor William of Orange, who had led a revolt against the Spanish Catholics in the northern part of the Netherlands. Frederick was not a successful a leader – his army was crushed by Habsburg troops in 1620. He fled to The Hague in Holland after the defeat and is known in history as the 'Winter King' because he had only been on the throne for one winter.

Comenius

In 1627, the Protestants were forced to choose: they must return to the fold of the 'true faith' (Catholicism) or leave their homeland. Around 150,000 people left the country. Among them was a man known as Comenius (1592–1670).

▲ *The Bohemian-born reformer Comenius.*

Comenius's real name was John Amos Komenský. He had studied theology in Bohemia and became a preacher, but he also had new ideas about methods of teaching – he wanted to see peace between people of different religions and he tried to achieve this by teaching his ideas in schools. When religious freedom was abolished in the Czech lands, Comenius fled to Poland, but his repuation was known across Europe, and he was invited to reform the Swedish educational system. In 1656 he was asked to continue his work in the Netherlands, and he moved to Amsterdam, where he stayed until his death. Comenius is an important figure in Czech history, as well as the history of several other European countries.

After the Thirty Years' War the power of the Habsburgs increased. The rich grew richer and the poor grew even poorer. It was only in 1740, when Empress Maria Theresa succeeded the throne, that several reforms were introduced to improve the situation. The empress encouraged freedom of religion and education for all. Learning German became compulsory and the Czech language was used less frequently.

Later, however, under Joseph II (who ruled 1780–90), teaching in Czech was allowed again and the power of the Roman Catholic Church was restricted. In this way, the Czechs had become more aware of their national identity – their own language and culture – by the beginning of the nineteenth century. The gap between the German-speaking and Czech-speaking people grew wider. Czech publishing houses were founded, which published books in Czech. Composers like Dvořák, Janáček and Smetana wrote Czech music, and a new national culture flourished once more (see page 30).

◄ *Leoš Janáček used traditional folksongs in his operas, which he wrote in his own language.*

Occupation and independence

In the later nineteenth century, industry began to develop in Bohemia. Many people moved from the country to the cities, and farming became less important as a way of life. During this time, the Czechs tried to gain self-rule, but they were unable to do so – the Austro-Hungarian monarchy was too powerful.

When the First World War (1914–18) broke out, Czech and Slovak leaders made a secret agreement, in which they planned a campaign for independence. After the war, the new state of Czechoslovakia was founded, which consisted of Bohemia, Moravia, Slovakia and a part of the Ukraine. The population was made up of 6 million Czechs, 4 million Slovaks, 3.5 million Germans and 700,000 Hungarians. Tomás Masaryk was made president of Czechoslovakia, and held the office until 1935.

In 1938, Hitler invaded Austria and claimed it as German territory. Bohemia and Moravia were next on his list. Resistance groups tried to prevent the invasion, but by 1939 Hitler's troops had occupied all the Czech lands, and the area became a satellite state of Germany, with the priest Joseph Tiso as its leader.

After the Second World War, the Germans were driven out of the region and Czechoslovakia became one country again under a communist regime supported by the Soviet Union. In the late 1960s, Alexander Dubček became secretary-general of the Communist Party, and allowed more political freedom. This period is known as the Prague Spring. It did not last long, and in 1968 Soviet troops invaded Czechoslovakia to re-establish Communism.

In November 1989, the Velvet Revolution – a bloodless uprising by the Czech people – put an end to Soviet dominance for good. Communism was abandoned and the first democratic elections were held in 1990.

On 1 January 1993, the Czech Republic and Slovakia became independent states. On 1 May 2004, both countries joined the European Union.

▼ Joseph Tiso, the nationalistic president of Czechoslovakia during the Second World War.

▲ Soviet tanks invade Czechoslovakia in 1968 to 'restore order' after the Prague Spring.

◄ A NATO meeting in Prague. The North Atlantic Treaty Organization was formed to preserve peace and international security between its member countries. The Czech Republic joined in 1999.

The country

The Czech Republic – officially called Ceská Republika – lies in the heart of Europe. To the west, it juts into Germany, to the south it borders on Austria, to the east on Slovakia and to the north its longest border – 658 km – is with Poland.

The Czech Republic is about as large as the Netherlands, Belgium and Luxembourg put together. Some 10.2 million people live there, in an area of 78,866 km². The population density is around 130 people per square kilometre. This is fairly low when compared with the population densities of other European countries – Holland has 466 people per square kilometre and Germany has 234.

Bohemia and Moravia

The Czech landscape can be divided into two regions: Bohemia in the north and west, and Moravia in the south and east. Bohemia is an area of lowland and rolling hills, surrounded by mountains, notably Šumava, a low mountain range with peaks of some 1,000 metres in height. In western Bohemia lie the Krušné Hory, the Ore Mountains, and in the north lie the Krkonoše, the Giant Mountains. Moravia is less mountainous. In the north and east lie the foothills of the Tatra Mountains, part of the Carpathian mountain range. The country's highest peak is Mount Snezka (1,602 metres) in the Giant Mountains. The lowest point – 115 metres – is near Děčín, on the River Elbe.

▼ *There are several lakes in the Czech Republic, most of which provide good fishing. This one lies in southern Moravia.*

▶ *The Vltava River flows past Orlik Castle in southern Bohemia.*

Rivers

Several rivers run through the Bohemian lowlands, including the Elbe (also known as the Labe) and the Vltava (or Moldau in German). The Elbe rises in the Krkonoše Mountains and flows westwards through the Czech Republic and Germany into the North Sea. The Vltava is the longest river in the Czech Republic – 434 km – and it flows northwards. The capital Prague lies on the banks of the Vltava.

The most important river in the Moravian region is the Morava. It flows from the north into the River Danube.

▲ *Spring brings a flurry of blossom and greenery.*

Forests

Forests cover nearly one third of the land in the Czech Republic. The most famous of these is the Bohemian Forest, in southern Bohemia, which is one of three national parks. The others are the Krkonoše (Giant) Mountains and the Podyji (see pages 45–46).

Climate

The Czech Republic is where Eastern and Western Europe meet and this geographical location is reflected in its climate. The western part of the country enjoys a moderate continental climate, with levels of rainfall spread fairly evenly throughout the whole year. The eastern part of the Czech Republic has a harsher continental climate – the summers are hotter and the winters colder. The mountainous regions generally experience more rainfall than the lowlands.

The Labe Valley in central Bohemia is the warmest region in the Czech Republic and has an average temperature of 7°C to 9°C. The river flows along a distance of 225 km through the Labe Valley. There is not much rainfall here – usually less than 500 mm a year.

Towns and cities

The Czech Republic's rich history is evident in nearly all the towns and cities, where many buildings from different eras have survived. Every year thousands of people flock to the country – and particularly the capital, Prague – to admire the architecture as well as to experience Czech customs and traditions.

Prague

Prague is situated on both sides of the Vltava River, and has a population of around 1.2 million. The capital of the Czech Republic is the largest historical centre in Europe, with over 4,000 monuments of historical interest. These include 80 churches, 70 palaces and over 100 historical gardens. Prague's city centre was once a number of different towns that grew and merged together, making up different areas of one large city. The old towns are Hradčany, Malá Strana, Město, Staré Josefov and Nové Město.

▼ *The Archbishop's Palace at Hradčany Castle in Prague.*

One of the most famous of Prague's monuments is Hradčany Castle, strategically situated on a hilltop overlooking the Vltava River. Work began on the castle in the ninth century. It was added to in later centuries, most notably by Charles IV (see page 8). Parts of the castle were destroyed by fire in 1541, but under Rudolf II (see page 9) it was repaired and expanded even further. Today it houses the offices of the Czech government.

In Prague itself there are many picturesque streets and squares. Perhaps the best known is the Staroměstké Námesti – the Old Town Square. Here, the main focus is the town hall, with its astronomical clock dating from 1490.

The 'Bridge of Eggs'

Once, the banks of the Vltava River were connected by no more than a narrow wooden bridge. In the fourteenth century, the people decided that they needed to replace the old bridge with a much sturdier stone one. The new bridge had to be indestructible, so they decided to strengthen the mortar by adding eggs, flour and honey liqueur. There were not enough chickens in Prague to provide all the eggs for the purpose so other cities in Bohemia and Moravia had to contribute their eggs as well. In some cities, when people heard of the request, they thought the inhabitants of Prague were starving and so they sent cheese as well. One town had a bright idea. They wanted the eggs to reach Prague without breaking and so, before transporting them, they boiled them all! Perhaps the plan worked and the eggs did strengthen it, because the Charles Bridge still stands strong and proud across the Vltava River.

◄ *People believe that touching this plaque means that they will one day return to Prague.*

▼ *The Charles Bridge, one of many bridges that span the Vltava. This footbridge is decorated with statues of saints, which were placed there in the seventeenth century. More statues were added in the nineteenth century.*

In the Old Town Square, many people have gathered with cameras and camcorders. They are waiting for the astronomical clock to strike 12. When this happens the statuettes will pop out of the clock. This is one of the most popular attractions in Prague.

'We knew it would take place around this time, so we made sure we could see it,' an onlooker explains.

The people wait excitedly for the clock to strike the hour. Suddenly the shutters burst open and the statuettes appear. A minute later, the spectacle is over.

▲ *The historic buildings in Prague are being carefully cleaned and restored.*

The old widow

Near the Loreto Church in Prague there once lived a poor widow. The woman had as many children as there were bells in the bell tower, so the people called the children the 'Loretta bells'. The widow wore a chain with a silver coin for each child. In those days there was an epidemic of the plague. The Black Death took all the widow's children, one by one. For each child the widow offered a coin to have the death-bell tolled, so heaven's gate would open up for the child. The widow herself was the last one to fall victim to this contagious disease. When she saw her own end approaching, she found consolation in the thought that she was going to follow her children to paradise. However, she had spent all her coins and there was no one to pay for the ringing of the bells for her. Suddenly, the bells started chiming of their own accord and they played a sweet song, as if angels were singing. Since those days the hour is not struck by a simple ring, but the chimes play a romantic melody.

◄ A daily fruit and vegetable market is held in Zelný Trh Square in Brno. In the middle of the square is a fountain, dating from 1695. The Museum of Moravia is on the far side of the square. The twin towers of St Peter and Paul's Cathedral can be seen rising in the background.

Brno

Brno is the second-largest city in the Czech Republic and the largest in Moravia. It has around 400,000 inhabitants. The city lies in a large valley surrounded by mountains on three sides. Its location at the meeting-point of the rivers Svratka and Svitava made it ideal as a stopping point on early trade routes and it grew in importance. It is an old city – founded in the tenth century – and over the years it has suffered damage at the hands of different attackers, including Swedes, Turks, Franks and Habsburgs; many of the old buildings have been destroyed or torn down to make way for new developments. However, the city is still an important centre of trade and industry. There are mines nearby, and Brno has a thriving textile industry.

A few older monuments survive, particularly those from the nineteenth century, when Brno was not only a key industrial centre, but also a scientific and cultural one, ranking amongst the finest cities in Europe in education and architecture. There are several universities and colleges here, including the College of Veterinary Medicine, the Janáček Academy of Fine Arts and the Military Academy.

Ostrava

Ostrava is the third-largest city in the Czech Republic and has about 320,000 inhabitants. It lies in the heart of the Moravian mining region and is a true industrial city. It began to grow in the 1830s and continued to develop when the railway was built from Brno to Vienna in Austria. Ostrava covers a wide area, but the city centre itself is quite small. It is mainly an important educational centre and is home to the college of mining.

► Liberty Square in Brno. The name dates from 1918, when the independent state of Czechoslovakia was proclaimed.

Plzeň

The Bohemian city of Plzeň has around 170,000 inhabitants, making it the fourth-largest city in the country. Its name is pronounced 'Pilsen', and the type of beer known as Pilsner was first made here. The city lies in an area where hops and sugar beet are grown. Besides beer, cars are manufactured here in the city's Škoda factory.

Plzeň is a very old city, founded in 1290 by King Wenceslas II of Bohemia, and it grew to become an important trade centre. However, it was not until the late nineteenth century that it became really industrialised, when the Škoda works were established.

The city was occupied by the Germans at the beginning of the Second World War and they used the factories and equipment available there to manufacture their armaments throughout the war.

Despite all this, there are several sites of historical interest in Plzeň. The town centre has a large square, the Náměstí Republiky, with several beautifully restored houses. There is also St Bartholomew's Church – built in the thirteenth century in the Gothic style – and the sixteenth-century town hall.

▲ *Ornate and colourful gabled houses line a square in Plzeň.*

◄ *One of the main streets in the industrial city of Plzeň.*

Olomouc

Olomouc is the fifth-largest city in the Czech Republic, with a population of about 100,000. It is situated on the Morava River and was once one of the most important towns in Moravia. Although Olomouc is an industrial city, it also has a large number of monuments, including the Cathedral of St Wenceslas, which dates from the twelfth century.

◄ *Parts of the old city wall in Olomouc are still standing.*

Domažlice

Domažlice lies in the west of the country, on the border with Germany, and is the capital of the Chodsko region. The Chods were a Slav tribe brought to this area by Duke Břetislav in 1040 to protect the trade route from Regensburg to Prague, and to fight off any invading Germans. In return, they were allowed to live as free men and women, and to hunt at liberty in the forest. The Chods sided with the Protestants in the religious wars of the seventeenth century and many of them were thrown in prison as a result. Their leader was hanged in the main square of Plzeň in 1625. The town still has many ancient buildings and is a fascinating place to explore.

Telč

Telč, a town in Moravia, has one of the most beautiful medieval squares in the whole of the Czech Republic. All the Gothic wooden houses that once made up the town were destroyed by fire in 1530; afterwards, the centre was completely rebuilt in the sixteenth-century Renaissance style. In 1992, the square was made part of UNESCO's World Heritage list.

▲ The church tower in Domažlice also served as a lookout point.

▼ The town square in Telč is surrounded by beautiful gabled houses in bright colours.

Slavkov u Brna – better known by its German name of Austerlitz – is a village of 6,000 inhabitants. In 1805, a battle was fought near here between Napoleon's army on one side and the Austrian and Russian armies on the other. The Austrians and Russians attacked with 86,000 men in heavy fog on the morning of 2 December. Around 8 o'clock the sun broke through and Napoleon managed to beat the allied forces. Tens of thousands of soldiers were killed.

▲ The sign welcoming visitors to the historic town of Slavkov u Brna.

▼ The fortress of Český Krumlov Castle towers over the rooftops of the town.

Český Krumlov

This historic town on the banks of the Vltava River in southern Bohemia is on the UNESCO list of World Heritage. It is one of the most visited towns in the Czech Republic because of its picturesque seventeenth-century centre, narrow streets and many squares with pavement cafés and restaurants.

◀ *The market square in Slavkov u Brna, near where the Battle of Austerlitz was fought in 1805.*

The town arose gradually around the fortress Český Krumlov, which was built on the bank of the Vltava River in the thirteenth century. The fortress towers high above the town. In the fortress gardens sits the Bellaria lodge, and nearby is an open-air theatre with a revolving stage.

According to legend, for centuries a white lady has haunted the fortress of Český Krumlov and the surrounding estates. From time to time she appears and makes a prediction. She is always dressed in a white gown with a veil. However, if she brings bad tidings, she wears black gloves. If a pleasant event is about to take place, such as a marriage or the birth of a child, her gloves are white. Nobody knows exactly who she is, but she was probably a member of the Rozmberk family, who lived in the fortress for many years. Some say she is the ghost of Perchta Rozmberk, the Count of Lichtenstein's wife.

The White Lady of Český Krumlov

In 1539, Jost Rožmberk's son Petr Vok was born in the fortress of Český Krumlov. The child was cared for by a wet nurse and a nanny. Both women slept in the nursery. Every night, when the fortress was shrouded in silence, the White Lady appeared at the cradle. If the child was crying, she would take it in her arms and rock it to sleep. One night, the wet nurse woke up. At once she recognised the White Lady, about whom so much had been told. The following night and the nights after that she kept watch with the nanny. As the ghost seemed to want to do no harm, the nanny was soon reassured and no longer stayed awake. But the wet nurse remained suspicious; one night she took the child away from the White Lady. The ghost disappeared through the wall and was never seen near the cradle again. When Petr Vok was a grown man, he heard the story of his mysterious nurse. He decided to tear down the wall through which she had disappeared. To his great surprise, behind the wall he found great treasures.

Martin and his friends are wandering around Kutná Hora. 'Look – second-hand books!' Martin exclaims, and rushes to the open chest standing outside an antique shop down a side street. His friends hurry after him. Martin takes out one of the books.

'What is it?' his friend asks.

'These aren't children's books, they're books for grown-ups,' Martin replies. He reaches deeper into the chest. 'A book on aeroplanes.'

'Let's have a look.' The three of them look at the pictures and dream about being pilots themselves and flying far away to distant lands.

Kutná Hora

Kutná Hora, in the middle of the Czech Republic, was once a wealthy city and was second only to Prague in terms of beauty and architecture. It gained its wealth from the silver mines that were scattered across this part of Bohemia – some were even in Kutná Hora itself. Around 1300, King Wenceslas II had the Royal Mint established in the town. This is where the Prague 'grosschen' – a silver coin – was minted. By the sixteenth century, however, the mines had been exhausted and the town's importance declined.

◄ ▼ *The St Barbara Cathedral in Kutná Hora is on the UNESCO World Heritage list. The road leading to it is lined with statues. The plaque below gives information about the site.*

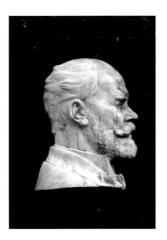

▲ *The spa town of Karlovy Vary attracts many tourists, who come to bathe in the therapeutic waters.*

Karlovy Vary

Karlovy Vary is spa town lying in the north-west of the country. The town was built on a river bank in a narrow valley and is surrounded by mountains. Because the river twists and turns as it flows, the town itself is also long and narrow. The medicinal springs were first used by Emperor Charles IV after he had been wounded in battle; he recovered very quickly after bathing in the spring water here, and the town is named after him – in German it is called Carlsbad. Many people come here, especially elderly people, who benefit from bathing daily in the waters.

◄ *The composers Smetana and Dvorák visited Karlovy Vary, and the Russian novelist Alexei Tolstoy also stayed here. The plaques commemorate these famous men.*

Celebrities have also visited Karlovy Vary, attracted by the medicinal springs, and the local fashionable lifestyle. Plaques appear on the buildings throughout the town, with the names of the famous people who have lived or stayed for a while in the town.

▲ A plaque marks the building where the Russian novelist Alexei Tolstoy stayed.

▲ This is the house where both the German writer Johann Wolfgang von Goethe and the composer Wolfgang Amadeus Mozart stayed in Mariánské Lázne.

Mariánské Lázne

Mariánské Lázne is another famous spa town, although it is much smaller than Karlovy Vary. It is surrounded by wooded hills and has a wide boulevard with many hotels, shops and restaurants. The sanatorium and the mineral springs are only a short distance from the town centre, in the middle of the woods. Here, too, many famous people have stayed, including the playwright Johann Wolfgang von Goethe, the composer Frederick Chopin, King Edward VII of Britain and Emperor Franz Joseph of Austria.

◀ A fountain in front of one of the bath-houses in Mariánské Lázne.

People and culture

The population of the Czech Republic is around 10.2 million. Eighty-one per cent of these (more than eight million people) are of Czech descent. Thirteen per cent, or nearly 1.5 million people, call themselves Moravian. In addition, there are about 300,000 Slovaks, 60,000 Poles and 50,000 Germans. The number of Roma (gypsies) is estimated at 100,000.

The five largest cities (Prague, Brno, Plzeň, Ostrava and Olomouc) together contain more than 20 per cent of the whole population – 25 per cent live in smaller towns and villages and 35 per cent live in cities with more than 50,000 inhabitants.

Roma people have lived in Central Europe for many years. Because they are nomadic – they move around rather than settling in one place – people didn't trust them. If a group of Roma settled near a village, the people there were afraid that the Roma would steal their children or use black magic to enchant them. Of course this was not true, but it gave the Roma a bad reputation. Discrimination is less widespread now than it used to be, but it still exists.

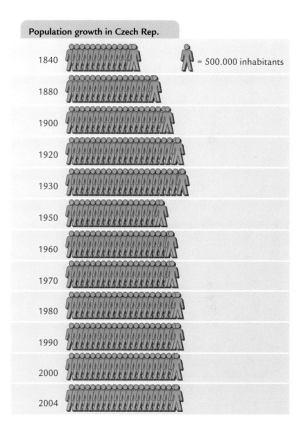

Population growth in Czech Rep.

1840
1880
1900
1920
1930
1950
1960
1970
1980
1990
2000
2004

= 500.000 inhabitants

▲ This chart shows the population growth in the Czech Republic since 1840.

◀ These girls are Roma, or gypsies. They are dressed in traditional clothing for the Roma festival that is held in Brno every year.

◀ *This Baroque church is in Velehrad; every August thousands of pilgrims flock to the town.*

Sudetenland Germans

For hundreds of years, Germans who were completely assimilated within the Czech population lived in Bohemia. This changed when Hitler came to power in Germany in the 1930s. The part of the population in Bohemia that was originally German became aware of its roots and the people decided they would rather belong to Germany. Hitler realised this gave him some support in Czech lands and in 1939 the German army simply marched into the country to annex the region. After the war, most of the 'Sudetenland Germans' (around three million) were sent to Germany.

▼ *A Protestant church in Velká Lhota.*

Religion

About 35 per cent of the population of the Czech Republic is Roman Catholic. Eight per cent is Hussite (see page 9). All other Protestant groups, such as the Lutherans, make up only 8 per cent. Almost 40 per cent of the population does not belong to any Church at all.

There was once a population of Jews in the lands that are now the Czech Republic. They arrived in the tenth century, from Germany and Hungary. The Czech people did not want the Jews living in their villages, so they were forced to establish their own settlements along the trade routes – mainly in the area around Prague's old town on the Vltava River (Josevof). The Jews in the Czech Republic suffered much persecution over the centuries, but the worst came in the twentieth century. When German troops invaded the country in 1939, thousands of Jews were deported to concentration camps in Germany and Poland, where many of them were killed. Only one third of the Jewish

◀ ▲ *Many reminders of the presence of the Jews remain in the Josevof Quarter in Prague, including the synagogue and the Jewish graveyard (above).*

population returned after the war. However, under the communist regime, they were not allowed to practise their religion, and many of them emigrated to Israel. By the end of the twentieth century there were only around 6,000 Jews left in the Czech Republic. The numbers of other minority groups have also declined since 1945.

Language

Czech is a Slav language, like Polish and Slovak. It uses the Latin alphabet, but some letters have diacritic marks (accents) over them. Vowels without an accent are pronounced short; long vowels are written with an accent. There are many words in Czech with a number of vowels in a row.

Some Czech words

Please	*Prosímvás*
Thank you	*Dekuji*
Hello	*Dobrýden*
Goodbye	*Nashledanou*
Yes	*Ano*
No	*Ne*
Sir	*Pane*
Madam	*Paní*
Soup	*Polévky*
Train	*Vlak*
Tram	*Tramvaj*
Street	*Ulice*
Market	*Trh*
Bridge	*Most*
Tavern	*Kavárna*
Swimming pool	*Koupalište*

▲ Guests raise the bride up in her chair at a Czech wedding reception.

Some Czech customs

M any Czechs in small villages have a large pitcher which they fill with beer in the local pub.

To make it clear that a woman is in the company of a man, he should enter first if they visit a pub or similar venue.

The first of May is Labour Day. If you are standing under a blossoming tree with a member of the opposite sex on May Day, you must kiss them. This is similar to the Celtic custom of kissing someone under the mistletoe at Christmas.

Wedding traditions

The Czechs have a number of traditions surrounding wedding celebrations. When the bride leaves her parents' home in the morning, she must put her right foot over the threshold first. This is believed to bring her luck.

At the wedding reception, a plate is thrown on the ground and then the bride and groom have to sweep up the pieces with a dustpan and brush. Keeping a single shard of the broken plate is also thought to be lucky. The wedding feast usually begins with soup. The bride's and groom's hands are tied together and they have to eat their soup with one spoon from one bowl.

The bride may be 'abducted' by the wedding guests, and then the groom must go out and search for his young bride. The bride is often taken to a pub, where the celebrations continue. If the groom finds her there, he has to pay the bill.

▲ A radio broadcast of a jazz festival taking place in Prague.

Media

The national broadcasting company, Česká Televize (Czech Television), has two transmitters, which broadcast programmes daily. There is also a commercial television station, called Nova. Most Czech television is based in Prague, although there are also studios in Brno and Ostrava, from which local programmes are broadcast. About 60 per cent of the programmes on Czech television are made in the country; the rest are imported. Not many of these foreign programmes are subtitled; instead, a person reads the lines in Czech, while the original version can be heard in the background. As in other countries, there is a lot of advertising on television.

There are over 150 radio stations in the Czech Republic; these include Radio KISS 98 FM, Impuls, Radio Frekvence 1 and Radio Europa 2.

Every year, Czech radio holds a drawing contest for children up to the age of 14. The subject for the drawing is a town or village in the area where they live. The best drawings are shown on a website: http://archiv.radio.cz/mapa/.

▲ *The castle at Červená Recice, drawn by Martin Pípal – one of the winning pictures in Czech radio's annual competition.*

The largest independent daily newspaper is *Mlada Fronta Dnes* which has a circulation of 425,000. *Blesk* is an independent daily tabloid and is printed in full colour. *Kvety, Refelx, Tyden* and *Mlady Svet* are weekly magazines.

▶ *As well as its own magazines, publications from other countries appear in Czech-language editions.*

Government

The country is a parliamentary democracy led by an elected president. Parliament consists of two chambers: the House of Representatives (Poslanecká Snemovna), which has 200 members chosen directly by the population, and the Senate, which has 81 members. General elections are held once every four years. The largest party in the Poslanecká Snemovna is the CSSD, the Czech Social Democratic Party, which won 30 per cent of the votes in the 2002 election. The second party is the ODS, the Citizens' Democratic Party, which gained 24 per cent of the votes.

◀ *Leoš Janáček.*

Music

The three best-known Czech composers are Antonin Dvořák, Bedřich Smetana and Leoš Janáček, all of whom composed during the nineteeth and early twentieth centuries.

Bedřich Smetana (1824–84) was born in Bohemia. He studied in Prague and became a teacher and pianist before starting to compose. His most famous orchestral work is a cycle of symphonic poems called *Má Vlast* ('My Country'), which is all about his native land. One of these poems, *Die Moldau*, has become particularly popular. Smetana's most famous opera is *The Bartered Bride*.

Antonin Dvořák (1841–1904) was born in the village of Nelahozeves, just north of Prague, and started his career as a viola player in the Prague Provisional Theatre orchestra. He later composed nine symphonies, a beautiful cello concerto, chamber music and operas, of which the fairytale opera *Rusalka* is the best known. His *New World* symphony has become one of the most popular concert works ever composed. Dvořák did not use traditional folk music in many of his works, but he has come to represent the Czech style of music more than any other composer.

Unlike Dvořák, Janáček (1854–1928) used many folk melodies in his compositions, and from his town of birth, Hukvaldy, he visited the surrounding mountain regions and wrote down the words and melodies sung by the local people. He also worked as a teacher and conductor in Brno. The opera *Jenufa* is his masterpiece.

In a park just outside the old town of Brno, 20 sculptors are at work. Lying before them are large sections of tree trunks, which they are cutting, sawing and carving. Several figures emerge from beneath their hands. The shape of a woman, an owl, a bear, a snake – even a king in his robes with a crown on his head. The sculptors also make wooden statuettes, which they sell to tourists.

Literature

The most famous Czech author is Franz Kafka (1883–1924). His books *The Trial*, *The Castle* and *Metamorphosis* have been translated into many different languages, and are known all over the world. Kafka lived in Prague all his life.

Another famous writer is Karel Čapek (1890–1938). *The War with the Salamanders* is his most famous book. Milan Kundera is the author of *The Unbearable Lightness of Being*, which is set in Prague, and which has been made into a film.

The former president of the Czech Republic, Václav Havel, was also a writer before he was elected to the presidency.

▲ *Franz Kafka.*

▲ *Czech author Milan Kundera's novel* The Unbearable Lightness of Being *has become a modern classic.*

A Czech fairy tale: The wood maiden

Once upon a time, there was a little girl called Betushka. She lived in a small cottage with her widowed mother. Every morning Betushka went to the birch forest to spin flax, as her mother instructed her, taking her two goats with her. She took with her a basket and a spinning top for the flax. In the afternoon she danced in the grass, for the nature that surrounded her filled her with joy. One day, a beautiful maiden approached Betushka, and asked if she could dance with her. Betushka agreed and they danced the day away, and the little girl forgot about her spinning. She did not dare tell her mother.

The next day, the beautiful maiden invited her to dance again. Only when it was growing dark did Betushka think of her empty spinning top. The maiden got the top spinning and within no time at all it was full. When her mother found the empty top from the day before she was angry, but her anger melted away when Betushka showed her the full top. The next day the maiden came again and once more they danced. Once again Betushka forgot her work, and became angry and sad. The maiden took the basket, disappeared and came back with it a moment later. Betushka was not allowed to look in the basket on her way home, but her curiosity got the better of her. The basket was filled with birch leaves. She threw some of them away, but then thought that the goats might like them. When she arrived home, her mother told Betushka that she had been given a magic spinning top that always remained full. Betushka remembered her basket and was startled when she looked in it: all the leaves had turned to gold! When Betushka told her story, her mother said that she must have met a 'wood maiden', who lived in the forest and sometimes abducted men whom they sought as husbands. The magic top made Betushka and her mother rich, and they lived happily ever after.

Education

Education in the Czech Republic is compulsory between the ages of six and 16, and is paid for by the government. Most schools are run by the state, although there are some private and a few church schools. All schools in the Czech Republic are co-educational (boys and girls are taught together).

▼ *These sculptures guard the doorway of a music school in Brno.*

Between the ages of three and six, most children in the Czech Republic go to nursery school, or kindergarten, where they play and get used to mixing with other children. Although this level of education is not compulsory, about 90 per cent of children go to kindergarten.

At the age of six children move on to primary, or elementary school. Here they learn reading and writing, as well as having basic lessons in science, in preparation for secondary school.

Secondary school, or high school, starts at the age of 10. Until they are 14 all children attend Junior High, where they are taught together. At the age of 14 they can choose between different types of high school. These include grammar schools, which continue a more academic education, or vocational schools, which train students for particular jobs. There are also special high schools for students who wish to concentrate their studies on art or music.

When they reach 16, students can choose to leave school and get a job, but almost all of them decide to stay at high school until they are 18. About 52 per cent of students start or continue vocational education, and around 48 per cent stay on in general secondary education. At the end of high school, they take exams which lead to a diploma, the *maturia*, which allows them to go on to higher education at college or university. Students must pass exams in four different subjects to gain their diplomas. Two are compulsory – the Czech language and one foreign language – and the others are optional.

The school year

The school year usually starts on the first Monday in September and ends on the last Friday in June. There are several breaks and holidays throughout the school year. The main holidays are at Christmas and Easter, which last about a week each, and a long break in the summer (around eight or nine weeks), but children also have days off, like Bank Holidays, for special occasions such as the winter festival or Liberation Day.

These girls attend a high school in Plzen. They have a day off today and are making the most of it by shopping in the town. They only have another year or so before they have to decide whether to leave school and get a job or to stay at high school until they are 18 and then go on to higher education. Most students in the Czech Republic decide to continue their education.

Higher education

There are 24 state universities and 12 private ones in the Czech Republic. The best-known and the oldest one is the Univerzita Karlova (Charles University) in Prague. The Masaryk University in Brno is also well-known. In Plzeň is the University of West Bohemia. There is also a college for agriculture and a university where students can study business administration and take management courses.

There are separate language schools for students who want to study foreign languages or train for a career as an interpreter.

◀ *The Charles University in Prague was founded in 1348 and offers courses in many subjects, including science, maths, medicine and theology.*

Cuisine

There are all sorts of restaurants in the Czech Republic, and just like in other European countries, it is easy to buy Greek, Chinese or Italian food. Hamburgers are also popular, particularly among young people. However, there are still many traditional Czech dishes on restaurant menus.

A Czech meal often starts with *polévka* (soup), which can be made from potatoes, chicken or cabbage. Many traditional soups are so thick and warming – often filled with vegetables, noodles and sometimes even a boiled egg – that they make an entire meal.

Meat

Main courses are usually made with meat. Pork and chicken are the most common meats used in Czech recipes. One of the most popular recipes is roast pork with dumplings. Main courses are usually eaten with potatoes or noodles. Coleslaw or tomatoes with some vinegar are often served as side dishes or in place of vegetables.

▲ *Sauerkraut with bacon is often eaten in winter in the Czech Republic.*

A popular side dish with meat is *knedlíčky*, which is made by mixing eggs, flower and white bread. The resulting dough is cooked in boiling water. When sliced, it is perfect for dipping in gravy or serving with soup.

Potatoes are always popular in the Czech Republic, and are served with meat or sometimes as a dish in their own right, in particular as a savoury potato pancake called *bramborák*.

Some dishes are associated with and cooked on special days and holidays. In Padubice, for example, people bake ginger cake in the shape of a heart, to celebrate their parish feast.

◄ *This soup uses* knedlíčky, *a bread-based type of dumpling that goes well with soups and gravy.*

▶ *Fishermen catching carp.*

Fish

The Czech Republic may not be surrounded by sea, but fish is still a popular dish. The rivers are teeming with different types of fish. The most common fish found in the country is carp, and there are many delicious recipes made with it, including a soup. It is traditional to serve carp on Christmas Eve. Trout, cod and mackerel are also caught locally.

Desserts

The Czechs enjoy rich desserts and use lots of butter and cream when making them. Traditional Czech desserts include pancakes, which are usually filled with jam and whipped cream, sweet dumplings made with fruit such as blueberries, and apple strudel. Ice cream is also very popular.

Recipe for houby s vejci (mushroom omelette)

Ingredients
1lb fresh sliced mushrooms
75g butter or margarine
1 teaspoon salt
1/4 teaspoon pepper
1/2 teaspoon crushed caraway seed
2 teaspoons chopped parsley
6 eggs, beaten

Sauté the mushrooms in the butter with salt, pepper, caraway seeds and parsley. When the moisture from the mushrooms has evaporated, stir in the beaten eggs until the mixture is firm.

Drink

Beer is very popular in the Czech Republic, and it is brewed in a number of cities. People drink an average of 150 litres a year. Most Czech beer comes from Plzeň (Prazdroj) and Ceské Budějovice (Budvar). Every September, a beer festival is held in Plzeň.

The Czech people also enjoy drinking wine, especially in Moravia, where a lot of wine is produced. In some areas, the hillsides are covered with vineyards.

▼ *Beer is an extremely popular drink in the Czech Republic.*

▲ *Grapes are picked in September or October depending on the weather.*

Czech beer

Beer was first brewed in Plzeň in 1842, but the history of beer actually goes back much further than this. Even before the Christian era, beer was drunk in Mesopotamia. Some 2,000 years before the birth of Christ, beer was presented as an offering to the goddess Nina. In that era, beer was also drunk by the Slavs in Bohemia. At this time, no hops were used in brewing – this thistle-like plant was only used as a raw material from the tenth century onwards. To prevent the excessive drinking of alcoholic beverages, towards the end of the eleventh century King Bretislav II introduced a law to discourage public drunkenness; he was also responsible for granting the privilege to brew beer. In spite of all the rules and regulations, beer brewers often quarrelled among themselves. Under Louis I, in 1517, a peace treaty was even signed to put an end to their fierce arguing.

Transport

The Czech Republic has a good transport system, mainly because its situation in the middle of Europe means a lot of traffic passes through for trade and other purposes. The roads and railway tracks are used as much as those in other European countries.

▼ *Trams are often the best way of exploring cities like Brno.*

Most of the roads in the Czech Republic are in a good condition and nearly all of them have been tarmacked. Occasionally there are holes in the road surface, caused by the increasingly heavy freight traffic. At railway crossings, in particular, this can be quite dangerous. The tracks often stick out above the tarmac, and drivers need to bump slowly over the tracks.

Before the Second World War, people in Czecho-slovakia drove on the left-hand side of the road, as they do in the UK. You can see this in the cars built before the war – which still exist in parts of the country – because they have their steering wheels on the right. The Germans changed this in 1939, and since then the Czechs have driven on the right-hand side of the road.

On some motorways, drivers have to pay a toll to use the road. At the moment, construction is underway on even more motorways, which will link the Czech Republic with other European road networks.

▼ *Even in the villages there can be a lot of traffic. The police regularly conduct speed checks.*

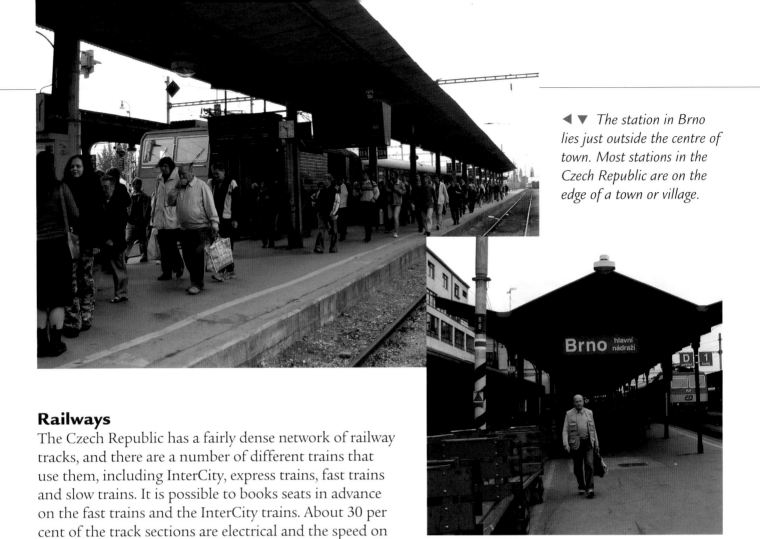

◀ ▼ *The station in Brno lies just outside the centre of town. Most stations in the Czech Republic are on the edge of a town or village.*

Railways

The Czech Republic has a fairly dense network of railway tracks, and there are a number of different trains that use them, including InterCity, express trains, fast trains and slow trains. It is possible to books seats in advance on the fast trains and the InterCity trains. About 30 per cent of the track sections are electrical and the speed on these is limited to 120 km per hour. There are plans to introduce a limit of 160 km per hour on the lines to Bratislava in Slovakia and Vienna in Austria.

The composer Antonin Dvorák had an unusual hobby: he loved trains. Nearly every day he would go to Prague station to watch the trains pass through. He would spend hours there and strike up conversations with engineers and station-masters. He wrote down the numbers and types of the locomotives in a little book. He also studied the timetables, so he knew by heart which locomotive was going where and what time it would reach Prague. One day he was unable to visit the station, so he sent his apprentice Joseph Súk to take down the numbers. Joseph was not as experienced as Antonin, and he made some mistakes – the composer was furious! He forgave Súk though, and Súk later married Dvorák's daughter.

Buses

Some cities have trolleybuses, which are propelled by an electric motor. The bus has two electric conductors that draw power from wires suspended over the street, as with a tram. Trolleybuses are better for the environment than ordinary buses – because they are electrically powered they do not release exhaust fumes.

Boats

Large parts of the River Elbe are navigable in the Czech Republic. From the port town of Chvaletice, the river has been turned into a series of canals along a 170-km stretch, making navigation possible even in times of drought. In this part of the river there are 21 locks. The second-largest port on the Elbe is Ústí nad Labem (Hamburg, in Germany, is the largest). The Vltava runs into the Elbe just beyond Prague.

Underground trains

Only Prague has an underground railway system. There are three lines, which run from 5 a.m. until midnight. It is a safe and quick means of getting around the city. Prague also has buses and trams.

▲ *Trolleybuses can be seen in many cities, and are an environmentally friendly method of transport.*

▶ *CSA is the Czech Republic's national airline.*

Aviation

The most important airport in the Czech Republic is Ruzyne, which lies 10 km outside Prague. Aircraft fly from here to many other European cities, and there are also domestic flights to Ostrava, within the Czech Republic. There are other airfields in Brno and Karlovy Vary, from which domestic and international flights leave.

The national air company is called CSA – Ceske Aeroline. This company owns 35 aircraft: three Airbus 310 planes for flights to Canada and the USA, and a Boeing 737 and 4000 for flights within Europe. For shorter flights they have smaller aircraft.

◀ *The underground rail system in Prague.*

The economy

The Czech Republic is known as a land of industry, and industrial areas and factories can be found all over the country. For centuries it has been an important trade route between different European countries, and it remains so today.

Near the mountains, around Plzeň and Prague, many different industries have sprung up. In the days of the communist regime, after the Second World War, all privately owned businesses and factories were taken over by the state, and the communist government decided what would be produced by them. Many people who had formerly owned small businesses found themselves having to work in factories. After the fall of the communist regime the situation improved, and industry is once again flourishing in the Czech Republic.

There is a great deal of heavy industry in this region. There are factories that produce machinery, locomotives, tractors, engines and cars. Škoda is the best-known Czech car and these are exported all over the world. The Škoda company is owned by the German Volkswagen group. There are also four nuclear power plants in the Czech Republic. There was strong protest when these were planned and built, but they remain active.

▼ *The Škoda plant near Plzeň provides many jobs and is one of the most important industries in the country.*

Mining

Mining has long been an important activity in the Czech Republic. For many centuries, the mountains in the areas where mining took place were known as the Ore Mountains. They stretch for a distance of 150 km along the German-Czech border. Mining has taken place here since the Middle Ages, when silver, copper, lead, iron and coal were discovered.

Although the supplies of many of the metal ores have now been exhausted, coal mining still goes on in the Ore Mountains. Coal is used as a fuel in electrical plants and blast furnaces. The mining has had an effect on the landscape, though. The area was once very clean and covered in forests – home to many plants and animals. Now it is dirty and barren.

▲ *The Czech Republic is famous for its glass-blowing and engraving, and for centuries there have been factories where mouth-blown glass has been produced. Today there are also factories where beautiful glass is made by machine.*

Currency

Although the Czech Republic has now joined the EU, it has not yet been decided whether it will adopt the euro. For the time being the Czech currency remains the koruna (CZK). There are around 44 CSK to one British pound, and about 30 koruna in one euro.

Batá

In 1894, Thomas, Antonin and Anna Batá started a shoe factory in the town of Zlín. By making their employees work at a conveyor belt, they improved on the normal levels of production of the time. By 1935 the factory was producing 25 million pairs of shoes a year. By 1938, there were over 65,000 people working for the Batá company. The family also opened shops to sell their shoes, and it was not long before the company had shops in 30 countries around the world. In many countries, homes and shops were built near the shoe factory for the workers. In the Netherlands, Batá bought some land near the village of Best, on which they built both a factory and houses for the factory workers in 1934. This complex is still called Batá Village. After the war, the factories in Czechoslovakia became state property. The name was changed to Svit and the Batá family emigrated to Canada. Now the old name is back and once again there are Batá factories and shops.

Agriculture

The communist regime also had an impact on the agriculture industry. In 1953, farmers were forced to hand over their property to the state, and they had to go to work on collective farms rather than managing their own land.

After the 1989 revolution, most farmers were given back their land. Today, about 70 per cent of farmland is used for crops. Major products include wheat, potatoes, sugar beet, cabbage and corn. Livestock, such as cattle, pigs and poultry, is still raised, but on a smaller scale. Timber is another important product in the Czech Republic.

Environmental issues

In the 40 years of communist rule, environmental issues were largely overlooked, and the effects of this neglect can still be seen. Power stations, which use coal for fuel, pour large quantities of sulphur dioxide into the rivers, and the polluted water is affecting the environment. The result is that many forests are slowly dying. The excessive use of chemical fertiliser has exhausted agricultural land in many places.

Environmental campaigners are trying to prevent further damage, and the government is introducing measures to help them. In many places, household waste is separated before being collected and recycled, and there is an increasing interest in sustainability.

▲ *Potatoes are an important food produced in the Czech Republic; they are harvested in the autumn.*

Tourism

Tourism is becoming an increasingly important part of the Czech economy. The country has a great deal to offer visitors from abroad, and although Prague remains the most popular destination, millions of people now travel to other parts of the country as well.

Most tourists travel to the Czech Republic by land. Of the more than 4.5 million people who visited the country in 2002, 94 per cent came by bus or car and 3.5 per cent by train; 2.5 per cent came by plane.

◀ ▼ *Castle Karlštejn, near Prague, was built in the fourteenth century by Charles IV, as a place of safekeeping for his treasures and crown jewels. It managed to withstand a siege by the Hussites that lasted for 24 weeks. The castle is one of the most popular tourist destinations around Prague.*

▲ *These girls are wearing the traditional dress of southern Bohemia. Tourists come to experience the many customs and traditions that have been revived since the decline of Soviet influence.*

▼ *The market square in Klatovy, in the south-west of the country. The city is famous for its catacombs, where the Catholic Jesuits are buried. The Jesuit church can be seen here with its two white towers.*

Most visitors to the Czech Republic come to admire the thousands of sites of historical interest in this ancient land. The country has over 2,000 castles and monuments and more than 40 protected cities.

The spa towns are another great tourist attraction. There are around 30 spas with thermal and mineral springs all over the country. Tourists and locals alike visit these to enjoy the water's medicinal properties.

Although tourists come for the Czech Republic's history, most find that the landscape is another great attraction. It is varied and beautiful in places, with its high mountains, dense forests and tranquil lakes.

Nature

The flora and fauna of the Czech Republic are similar to those in most Central European countries, but like the landscape itself, the plants and animals found here are quite diverse.

▼ *Brightly coloured flowers grow among the moss on the rocks.*

Trees and plants

Around 30 per cent of Czech land is covered in forest. On lower ground these are usually made up of birch, maple, oak, chestnut and ash trees. In the more mountainous regions, pine, fir and larch trees grow.

In the grasslands, where the soil is very rich and the climate is warm, many rare flowers flourish.

National Parks

There are several areas in the Czech Republic that have been designated protected areas. In north-eastern Bohemia, on the border with Poland, lie the Krkonoše – the Giant Mountains. This is a low range with peaks reaching to around 1,500 metres, and with deep valleys and steep slopes. This region is popular with the Czechs because it has much to offer all year round. In the winter, people go cross-country skiing or walking in the snow; in the summer there are many good hiking trails.

The Krkonoše National Park is also known as Ceské Švýcarsko – 'Czech Switzerland'. The Kamenice River flows through this area, and eventually runs into the River Elbe. The river has carved deep canyons into the rock, creating a mountain landscape that looks similar to those found in Switzerland, hence the park's name.

◀ *The landscape of the Krkonoše National Park is rather like that of Switzerland, with clean air, pine woods and green valleys.*

The Šumava National Park is one of the largest in Europe. Most of it is covered by the Bohemian Forest, in the western part of the Czech Republic. The woods stretch out into Germany, where they are known as the Bavarian Forest. As well as the woods, meadows, hills and lakes are common this area. It is very popular with cyclists.

The third national park in the Czech Republic is the Podyji National Park, which lies on the border with Austria. The park extends across the border, and the Austrian part is known as the Thayatal National Park. The area has grown up around a river valley, and is largely made up of woodland, with small non-wooded areas. The fact that this park crosses a border between the two countries means that there has been a great deal of co-operation in maintaining its beauty.

▼ *The Bohemian Forest is popular with walkers and cyclists.*

Animals

The country's different landscapes are home to various types of animals. Deer are common in the forests and on the borders of fields. Foxes can also be found here, although because of their shy nature they are not often seen – they only leave their dens at night to go in search of food. The lynx, a type of wildcat, is rare, but it does make its home in the forests of the Czech Republic. Wild boar can be seen frequently. Boars cause problems for the farmers because they dig up the fields with their snouts while looking for food.

Birdlife is also plentiful in the forests, particularly songbirds. The lakes are home to ducks, swans and many other water birds.

The stork is a common sight near houses and farms. Many people who live in the countryside put up high poles with old cart wheels or dishes on top for the storks to build their nests on.

Birds of prey like the buzzard and the falcon are common, although eagles and hawks are rare in the Czech Republic.

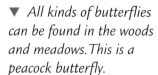

▼ *All kinds of butterflies can be found in the woods and meadows. This is a peacock butterfly.*

▼ *Geese ready for take-off.*

Fish

There are plenty of fish in the rivers and lakes. Carp are the most abundant, but there are also trout and pike. There are many fish farms in the Czech Republic, where fish are bred 'in captivity'.

◄ *Park rangers take tourists and schoolchildren on tours of the forests. They know the best places to see the wildlife and where the rare plants grow.*

Glossary

Celts A number of different tribes from Central Europe, who had the same language and cultural roots.

Franks A west Germanic tribe who settled in Europe in the area mostly covered by present-day France.

Gothic An ornate style of architecture dating from the Middle Ages.

Habsburg Empire The land under control of the German royal family, who gained the thrones of several countries, including Bohemia, from the late Middle Ages to the twentieth century.

Hussite A person who believes in the Protestant religious reforms put forward by John Huss.

Middle Ages The period from around AD 500 to 1450.

NATO North Atlantic Treaty Organization, established in 1949 to work towards security and co-operation between the member states.

Orthodox Church The Christian Church in the East, with several independent sects.

Slavs A large group of European people with similar languages. Individual tribes descended from the Slavs include Slovaks, Czechs, Poles, Serbs and Croats.

Stone Age The earliest period in technological history, when tools and weapons were made from stone.

Teutons Ancient tribes of Germanic and Scandinavian origins.

Theology The study of religion.

Index

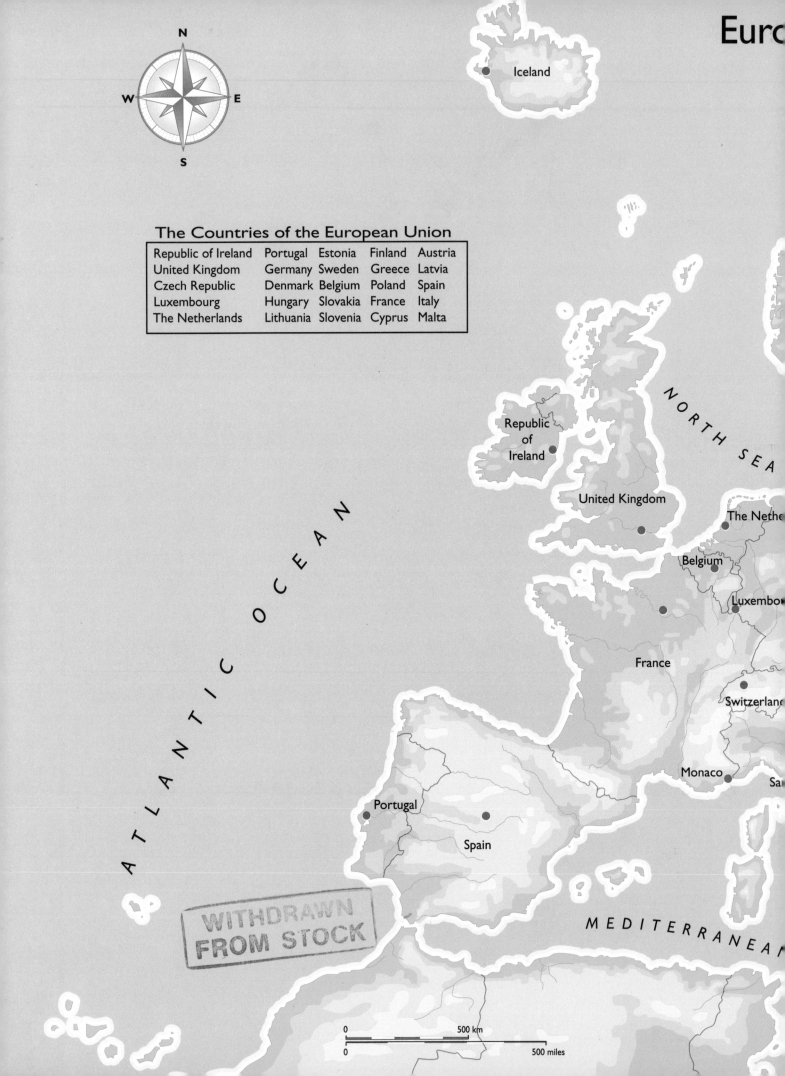

Eur

Iceland

The Countries of the European Union

Republic of Ireland	Portugal	Estonia	Finland	Austria
United Kingdom	Germany	Sweden	Greece	Latvia
Czech Republic	Denmark	Belgium	Poland	Spain
Luxembourg	Hungary	Slovakia	France	Italy
The Netherlands	Lithuania	Slovenia	Cyprus	Malta

NORTH SEA

Republic
of
Ireland

United Kingdom

The Nethe

Belgium

Luxembo

France

Switzerland

Monaco

Sa

ATLANTIC OCEAN

Portugal

Spain

MEDITERRANEAN

0   500 km

0   500 miles